On Chasing Dragons and Other Topics

2nd Edition

For Grace

☆

For it is in giving that we receive,
it is in pardoning that we are pardoned,
and it is in dying that we are born to eternal life…

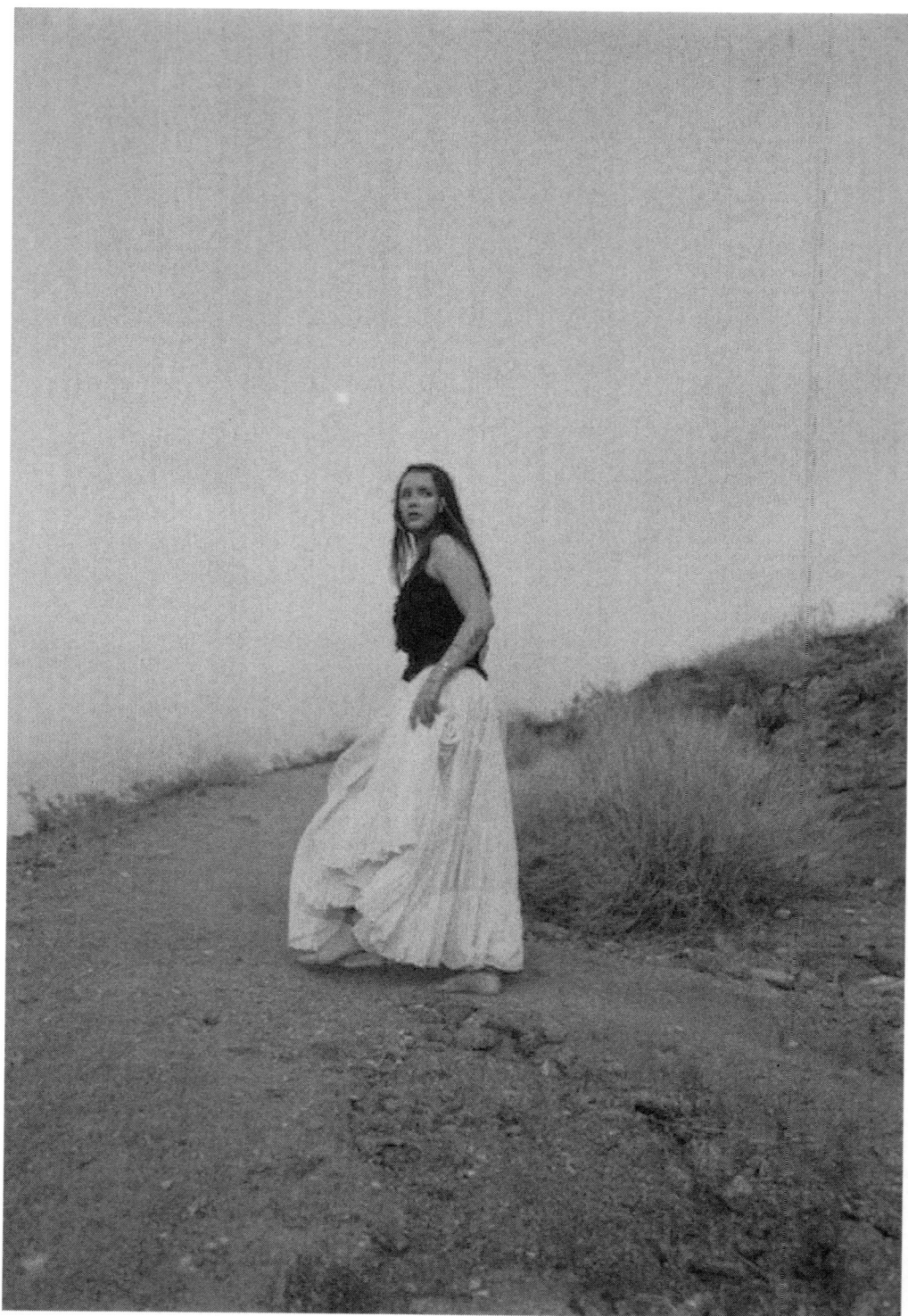

Arrive! On Chasing Dragons and Other Topics- A book of my earliest poems, Written across the span of one hundred lifetimes. Inspired by trials and tribulations in the City of Angels, a string of dead-end love stories, dead lovers, and living a life forged of beauty and poison.

Ophelia

Trailer park on a river - Northern California

We were calm as the water rose,
It won't reach us
Frog legs in the winter? What an uncommon request,
 But a request nonetheless
Milk of amnesia was served on the side, as a refreshment
The devil girl on the trailer never stopped staring at me.
Did her clothes make her an advocate? Or was it her eyes?
It was her eyes I'm sure of it.
"Donde Vives?" she said
We couldn't answer
"I'm going to help you if I can"
But our words had become profound, complex, and involuntary
"If you grew wings you would be an angel"
Who said what we were unsure, but we knew it was only a matter of time before she
became a victim of my merciless imagination
The garden had flooded
Jesus was a vampire and ruler of the bees
9 candles form a fire and the harnessed flames come to my aid in an attempt to rescue my
kidnapped solace
Lizard Brain
Suffering and stuttering
between the clashing consciousness of attraction and anguish
United we stand, divided we fall...

Hollywood, Fuller Apartment

The vital part
The essence fastened inside me
Four chambers suspended within a cage
I am unable to distinguish your condition
For I am afraid you have perished,
Have you been so lucky to have found oblivion?
I must call into question 'rebirth' and the likelihood of it finding you

Hollywood Freeway, Back of a Jeep

My laments engulf me
I am immersed in a cool fog that speaks in languages of desolation
Eternal bleakness
My heart is voiceless and its notions fall distorted
My wills and principles have disfigured,
Allowing these familiar conclusions to be written
within me
All irrevocable
They form a senseless nonexistence
It is because of time; the inevitable healer
That decay transpires and the earth claims what we believed was ours

Hollywood & Highland

I remember the psychosis
Time & gravity both phantoms of this plague nurtured within me
An elixir internal
Its presence, perpetual

The visual memories
Blood from the junkies stain the sidewalk-
this winter's first rainfall
The ramblers
The drifters
I stand atop the building , all forms of my body Flooded by intoxication and inspiration
Each a product of the other
Luxuriating in an orgy of violence
The promise of a thousand deaths sustains me

Is it wretched
That one such as I
Often relish in and find life
In torturous death
The maker of years
Love sessions
Erotic politicians

My name is progress and you are decay

Laney College, Oakland

We spoke of oleander and resurrection,
We spoke of atomic theory and the quixotic fear of all things beastly that blossom within us,
All of us
To deny these ideations is to deny oneself
Shutting out and blackening half of the mind,
Dismantling the fragile harmony of wholeness
The comprehension that being and non-being produce each other

Pasadena

Apprise me of your daydream
my mind is open to tell of your perception The perception of I
Who was I?
A muse forged of bourbon and blue pills
I built castles in air
Morphine
Twink
Manifesto
My name is Sinatra and I will perish for you
For you named me
My everything
with cigarette exhaust and burnt sienna
surely, love is apothic and that we see the same

Even the tragic beauty must grow old

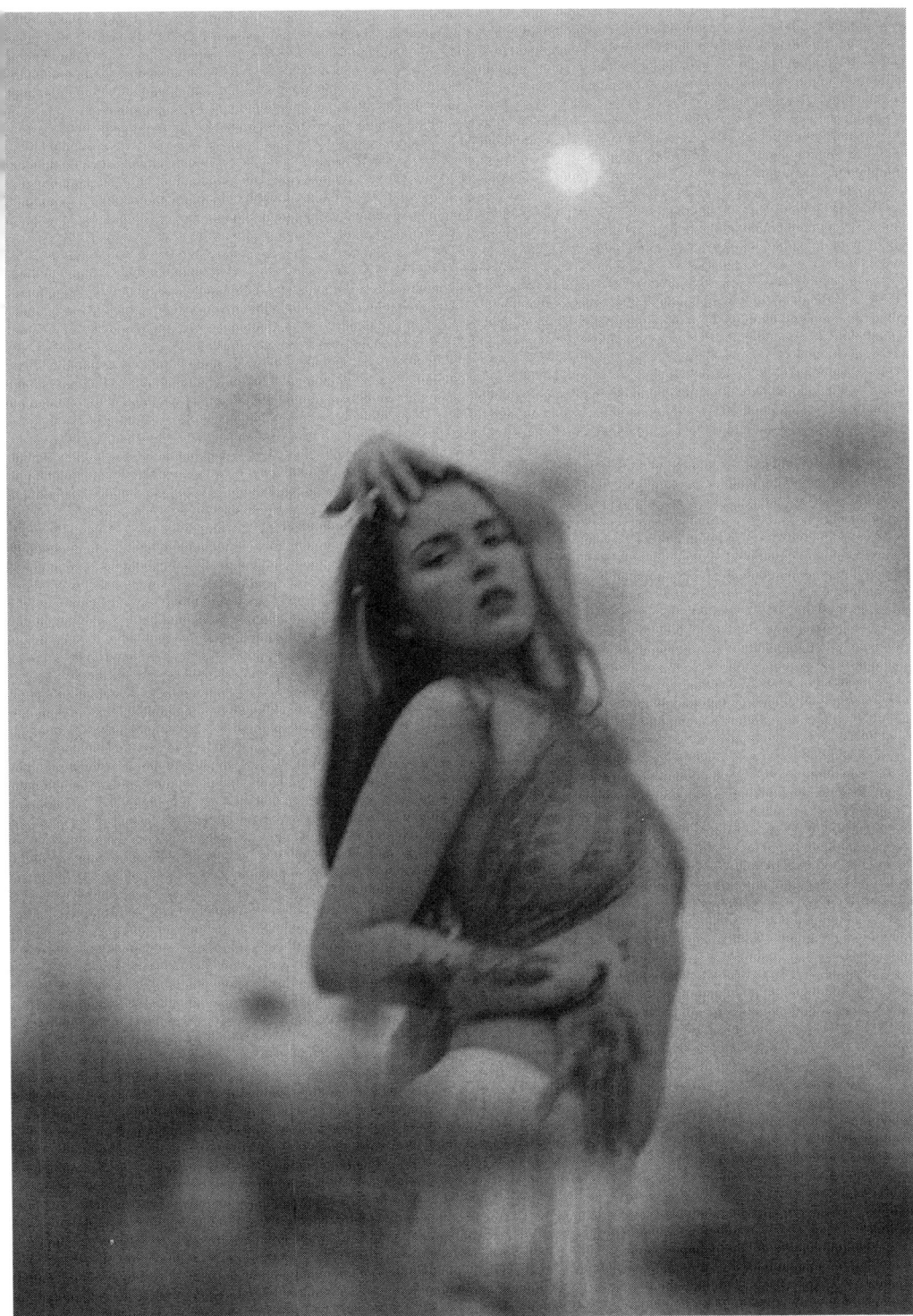

16

Airplane, LA to Sacramento

A lamb
I am directed vigorously
I am lured to the slaughter
yet I ask no questions
The enigma that is my mind
perpetually manifesting freedom through oppression the art in my beauty, and the beauty
in art
perhaps, interchangeable
but at what cost must this come so easy?
the pain - exquisite
the instant release I have been robbed of
an internal comfort that burned warmer than the sun a one sided love
that falsely peddled me the gift of purity
perhaps then,
I am not pure

The Oakwood

I am hollow with space inside
Dark sky breeds warm air and upholds my composure
It is serenity - with blood
I cry for all my men my children my home as Grace fills the strawberry sky
Your hands
my hair
shining palm chandeliers
What will you be without me?
For me without you is a question that visits often

San Francisco i died within you Your motel 6, strip club brothels, 3 am
Friends with the city rats,
Eating bread off the park bench
and coke off your streets... High at the art gallery
The men were cruel
And you never loved me
I'm reminded of your pain when i think of your lights

Palm desert you gave me many lovers
Though never any to keep
Remember the year when Snow met your palms?
That year became many
Ecstasy, salt water pool, can I get a ride with you?
The kids who had it all
Everything kids
Leaving our problems to find new ones
Your sun burns my skin, come find me next spring
Forget the lovers

Los Angeles you named me Opulence
Your hills, a portrait my face, body structure
Fragile and charming
I remember the life we spent together
You were sugar, and I, roses
Joyous & free, my heart & my keeper
I remember the day you changed your mind, your air turned blue and bitter
The sun blackened to never return
Pico Union left me for dead...

Our last night together at the Roosevelt, two lovers and drugs in the bungalow

Then, You pushed me out
...How dare I ever leave you?

RV park

I've found them; the days of rest
They do nothing but expose the tongue of unrest Stop crying
Stuck on me like a fucking flea
This headache means my brain is withering
Withering means to perish

On Love that didn't last

You call for me and I am delivered to you under the moonlight
Upon an altar you set me gently
This night begins like all the others
Naked Worship
Turpentine & sienna
Soft white Plumerias drift from the skies,
they adorn my golden hair
The blue Smoke travels, arises from my mouth
our eyes meet, and for a moment you love me
You are the darkness from which I glow within and I glow only for you

I remember my first love
An attraction so persuasive,
Debilitating
A trance of mystics and magics
Both time and space elapse before you
The emotional body, in its damage, takes over
To ascertain up from down?
A challenge for kings
Yet kingdoms will collapse for you
For you
Minds become mindless
Take heed of my instructions
So you may learn from my misfortune

Oakland Hills, in a dream

White Russia

Have I died enough times to make you miss me?
Does this not pain you as much as that?
And in turn, no difference is felt here nor there?
No proclamation enlightens me quite like reverence and your reverence past
Does nothing remind you of the past?
It is everywhere I turn
Perhaps I live in fear for reasons I cannot share
They speak softly
Open the doorway
Step outside
You don't see the sun go down

And I have scattered myself among men and women along the way

Death Valley, California

Cars pass by
Humping the road
Birds of death
the crow,
lands on the hill to eat the dead
For depraved are the eyes
that look toward the church
Golden hair
the wind combs you
World famous delights on a soft Easter morning
The sun isn't here yet
It asks us to wait
time has no weight here and that is the delight

How many times will I die for you?

The Oakwood

This is the part where clarity finds me. Ten days later, on my back ,
fatigued
I remembered my legs were once strong in good condition.
O vindictive lover, I sought in you forgiveness, but you are unforgiving ..
My secret renaissance,
I am, adopted and betrayed by you
You -
A specific strain of both violence and ego.
I have been warned of you to far extents . .
Perhaps I've fallen deaf

Pacoima, California

I remember grasping it all
I had spent all this time with my vision distorted and backwards
caught up in violent lust
rotten obsessions fueled me
& my junket toward the danger zone
Into hell
where others are blind to my good intentions
I live under the house of man
Where fate has banished me into the abyss that is fear itself

Los Feliz

I am torn apart
ripped limb from limb
the pieces left behind,
my wings undusted, peeled, ripped from my body
How disruptive
the blade's performance
and my glory, deconstructed
this pain revolves around you
you deliver it unto me
dare I call it an act of grace
yet you claim to be the giver of such graces
graces and charms
but neither grace nor charm can withdraw me from you

My soul cries for purity and to be familiar with her...

1209 S Lake Street, Pico Union

I have seen the devil
I have seen him many places
Scattered along the way
No more than a moment, a flash
He is in the eyes of an angry lover
Recoiled
He is in every sip, swallow, plunge.
Every exhalation
He is in the darkest corners of the world waiting
He knows your name
He knows you love to feel

And few of you have
Or ever will experience
How painful it is
To have your soul again enter your body

The Vampire's Apartment

The fear of the people is fueling this war
Playing musical poisons
they wait for you to want it
The way a cigarette tastes after you've cried for hours
True north
of forms and phenomena
Today's pain is different from yesterday's
X111

I5 Freeway

My life here is dynamic
My interactions with others - lively
speaking to and thinking with them
New souls poured into bodies sent before me I greet them with acclaim and warm regard
but at the end of the day I'm alone
And the end of the day comes often

Nocturnal joyrides
Amtrak veteran
It's where many men go for a nice night in Alabama
Tigers lungs
Frozen water, monkey mind
Salvation lies within
My body is the map of America
My body spells trouble in paradise
My body will ask you;
When do you feel most free?

To all the pretty girls in LA

I love the way you're cool in the face of despair
I dream about your heavy eyelids, designer parfum, tangled hair
To the dirty girls from Hollywood La Brea, who are empty, counting calories
To the street cats that fall from balconies
I love the way you undress your shitty tattoos
I imagine the story behind each one, underage, drunk on plastic bottle booze
Eating up false promises from those who claim they understand you
Going low to get high, where the drugs are free, the stories are true
I've known you for years yet you're interchangeable, easy & fast
Escapism, tweak, no sleep, plagued by your past
I've met enough of you to know that you'll always choose men instead of each other
Whether the money is right or not at all
Crass, lucky, living off friends, forsaken by your mothers
I love the way you pull yourselves together, public bathroom, 4 more days to pick up the pieces
Pretty little heads full of suicidal ideations, the art of finding drugs, the art of letting go
I love you when you drink whiskey on the train with the friends in your head
7 pm and you've had too much because you've told him your name was Jasmine
I love the way you say my name, always hopeless and in tears
Sweet desperate voices, the drugs have left you, brace for the fear
Who do you see in the mirror when you lie to yourself? Will it be different this time?
I love how you'll never know who real friends were, or what years hurt you the most
Or how for the rest of your lives, you'll always remember the men who fed off your youth and called it love

Hollywood Roosevelt pool

Indulge in your past, remember it fondly cherish the darkness
It lives within you, sleeps within you
Now light fills your chamber
Come forward from the stream of life
The miracle of water and nature itself
Muted expressions, your accent lingers & love lingers
I am nicotine, I am power
"Come back to me" twinkles the city I long for your grit
your spirit awakened me years ago
Drink from the stream, my loved one
milk, elixir entirely born from the stream Embellish your life, adorn it with care, with
chaos And with vigor
Success and its surrender
Surrender accordingly
My child you are divine timing...
it was written in the stars

Do you remember how I loved you?
How deep you ran within me
Your blood within my blood
Your sun bleached hair and golden skin
Each freckle and its containing constellation
Pissing in bottles
Rams aflame on mars
Your fire scorched my earth until it was black
Cursed to live an eternal summer
But when I was swimming beside you in God's great ocean I could forget the way you'd
rage
The way you'd destroy me without lifting a finger

the soil, the flesh of the earth

the earth and
roots contained within
the earth

succumb to

bear, tolerate, endure

unable to differentiate ~~sta~~ b/t
My heart — the vital part
the essence
cant tell if my heart
is dissapeared or just destrajed
call into quinnregeneration.

unable	precieve	entirely
inadequate	understand	vanish
unfit	differentiate	perish
powerless	distinguish	pass into oblivion
incapable		impossible to find

(1.18) cryptic   high-born
unprincipled   anguish, trauma
detach   outlaw
extrasolar   ~~exalt, eternalize
vulnerable   on the run
'game of chance'   lambskin
opulent   ~ fortune teller
                    dismal,

mom
de-slick spray

video matches words ✓

(11·21)

different ~~pauses~~ pauses + new lines = pic/video of words

the mass of me + my entirety suffers
without you.
lamb. [sheep drawing] (actual and frame) I am directed vigorously.
I am lured to the
slaughter, I ask no questions. ~~question~~
~~nothing~~. the enigma that is my mind
perpetually manifesting freedom by/thru oppression
the art in my beauty and the beauty in
art. perhaps interchangeable
but At what cost must it come so easy?
~~the exquisite pair of~~
·the pain exquisite, ~~it is surrounding/~~
~~the noose~~ luxuriating within me.
removing it? an easy fix-
the instant release i have been robbed of.
an internal ~~warmth~~ comfort that burned
warmer than the sun. ———— falsely.
a one sided love that peddled/offered/~~gifted~~
me the gift of purity awarded/gave/
perhaps, I am not pure?
mon

HEAD HIGH
BODY HIGH
PEACHS PENTHOUSE
LIFE'S A PEACH
MEMENTO MORI
NICOTINE DREAM   "TEEN DREAM"
THE ART OF LETTING GO
OPIUM / MORPHINE
VIPERIDAE
CARPE NOCTEM
CUI BONO?
VOX NIHILI
AMOR VINCIT OMNIA
ETERNAL LIFE

it is because of that
time; the inevitable. decay comes
and the earth claims
what we, believed was, ours.
vines entwine; lacing ~~that~~ once
~~in~~ our trespasses
buildings and bridges, sheathed
for she is forgiving.
in the spirit of forgiveness,
the trap houses and churches alike.
willingly accepting the wanderers,
the adders, those who abandoned.

in language only
sheathed
in her
forgiveness

my laments engulf me,
I am immersed in a cool fog
that speaks of desolation.
constant | eternal bleakness
My heart is voiceless, ~~cold~~ and
it's notions are distorted.
My wills and principles have disfigured
~~to ready to~~ allowing these malignant
conclusions to be engraved.
all irrevocable,

Baudelaire
Gravida

the erotic must always be ugly,
the aesthetic always divine,
and death always
        beautiful.
                dali

capacity   papaver somniferum
antediluvian   diacetylmorphine
odyssey   crepuscular ray
haunt, consume, plague
neurosis   petrichor - rain smell
pale, alabaster   sastruga - snow formed by wind
magnificent
pedantic, purist
perpetual, everlasting, undying
phantom
placid, tranquil
elixir

the visual memories
the ramblers
the drifters
overwhelmed and flooded by
intoxication and inspiration.
each product a product of the other
luxuriating in an orgy of violence
the promise of 1000 deaths sustains me

trashed all greviences

we are souls not caught under
time or space

death is taking off a tight shoe

suffering is grace
being in the presence of death
= presence of truth

vehicle of awakening
god comes to the hungry in
the form of food

NO line of advance in any
particulak direction
can be traced

free activity and
childs play

my rehab is full of
frogs
    But i like when the
air smells of burnt tobacco

(search up the cigarette
ingredients)

benzene + Butane
    the distant music echoes
down   the dirt road —

the water boils

    the mountain and her
trees

disorder
blood-shed
solace
revival/downturn
renaissance
'Kill all hopes'
mourning dove
good-condition/wellness
chest pain

Teaching trades thru
observation.

A SPECIFIC STREAK OF
violence
ACID eat.

IN a WORLD WHERE TRUTH
is seen as beauty.

PERPETUAL

MISFORTUNE
MISFIT

LOSSES-FOES

Lapsed

mourning doves

i have seen the devil
i have seen him many places.
scattered along the way —
who more than a moment, a flash
he is in the eyes of an angry
lover

recoiled

~~he habituates within~~
~~drink~~ ~~drugs~~ ~~people~~ he comes with

with
promises of
entertainment

~~we are weakening~~

drugs - white noise
breakdowns
psychotic / neurosis
rats, mold
sinister
absence of god

providing these
~~we~~ synthetic feelings

in places

this winter is cold
but I am
colder

waiting for you/us/me
where he knows
I will find him

he is in the darkest/corners of the world
he is in every pull, swallow, plunge
every exhalation
he fills our lungs, our needles and
kill the body and head will die
he knows your name and your
favorite feelings.

floating/
numb but I feel.

I feel nothing but I feel it deep
I feel nothing and I feel it deeply deep

my soul cries for
purity
&
to be
familiar with her

my sorrows learned to swim

the sunset, my pacifier

the cement steaming
as the rain falls

the rain falls steady
sun shines into my eyes

grateful for my sleep

transgressions

tolerance

Diencephalon = thalamus + hypothalamus

A.

T

HP

M.B

ir

O

P

B.

ST

T — DORSAL THALAMIC NUCLEUS &
large egg part of thalamus
majority of thalamus

INTERMEDIATE MASS   A √√
small, round point at
median of thalamus

PINEAL GLAND A √
small, round, above "6 pack"
posterior side, medial
source of melatonin

Hypothalamus — √
PITUITARY GLAND B √
sits in sella tursica

INFUNDIBULUM B
canal connecting P.G
and hypothalamus

MAMMILLARY BODY below (dia A) √
inferior to hypothalamus

thalamus — sensory processes
hypothalamus — motor processes

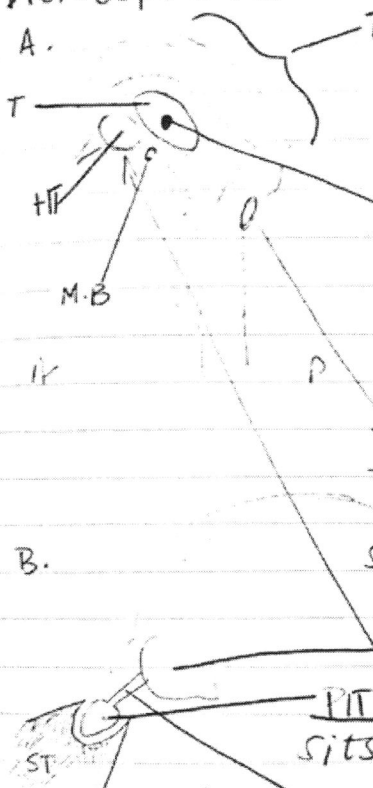

my life revolves around
5 pm

2·20·18
THIS IS THE PART WHERE
clarity finds me.

    ten days later
on my back
        frail
        (fatigued)
        weak
        ailing
my legs were once strong and
    in good condition
my vindictive lover . . . I sought in
                              you - forgiveness,
but you are, unforgiving

    my secret renaissance, your name
traded me
        a specific strain of both violence
and ego, I have been named
of you to far extents.

        Lost in the Truth

perished
amity lintamooj   malignant, paradox
                Bacchus-
        intoxication + inspiration

assisted
suicide   ⊗ lament
                    passionate expression of
                    grief or sorrow
                    ⊗ words like wanderers
                                the___ers? vagrant
                                            ·adders
                                biblical

wanderers   those who left
whispers   ran
                            abandoned

        visual memories memory

rambiers   we who divided
drifters   diverging from

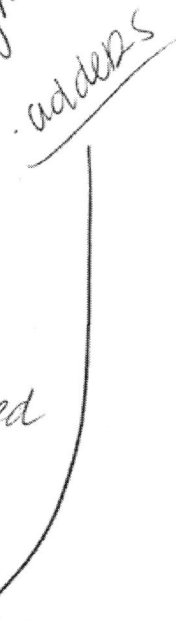

3·7·18 2:17 PM WED

i REMEMBER GRASPING IT ALL,
I HAVE SPENT ALL THIS TIME
WITH MY VISION DISTORTED
AND BACKWARDS CAUGHT UP
IN VIOLENT LUST, ROTTEN
OBSESSIONS FUELED' ME/MY'
THIS JUNKET TOWARD THE DANGER
ZONE, + INTO HELL.
WHERE OTHERS ARE BLIND
TO MY GOOD/PURE INTENTIONS,
I LIVE UNDER THE HOUSE OF
MANI, THIS IS WHERE MY FATE HAS FOUND/
ME, BROUGHT ME/ HAS BALLISTED
ME INTO THE/ ABYSS THAT IS FEAR
ALL ITSELF

♡

Ophelia

Printed in Great Britain
by Amazon